TRIANGLE HISTORIES

THE CIVIL WAR

# ULYSSES S. GRANT

**David C. King**

BLACKBIRCH PRESS, INC.

WOODBRIDGE, CONNECTICUT

Published by Blackbirch Press, Inc.
260 Amity Road
Woodbridge, CT 06525
Web site: http://www.blackbirch.com
e-mail: staff@blackbirch.com
© 2001 Blackbirch Press, Inc.

Printed in China

10 9 8 7 6 5 4 3 2 1

**Photo credits:**
Cover, pages 4, 6, 17, 18, 19, 30, 32–33, 34, 35, 36, 68, 90: ©North Wind
Picture Archives; cover (inset), pages 13, 16, 20, 26, 39, 40, 46–47, 54, 58,
59, 60, 62, 65, 80, 82, 94, 95: The Library of Congress; pages 9, 75:
National Archives; pages 10, 99: National Portrait Gallery.

**Library of Congress Cataloging-in-Publication Data**
King, David C.
Ulysses S. Grant / by David C. King
            p. cm. — (The Civil War)
Includes index.
            ISBN 1-56711-555-1 (alk. paper)
1. Grant, Ulysses S. (Ulysses Simpson), 1822–1885—Juvenile literature.
2. Presidents—United States—Biography—Juvenile literature. 3.
Generals—United States—Biography—Juvenile literature. 4. United
States—History—Civil War, 1861–1865—Campaigns—Juvenile litera-
ture. [1. Grant, Ulysses S. (Ulysses Simpson), 1822-1885. 2.
Presidents. 3. Generals.] I. Title. II. Civil War (Blackbirch Press)

E672 .K55 2001                                        2001002043
973 . 8'2'092—dc21

# CONTENTS

# PREFACE: THE CIVIL WAR

Nearly 150 years after the final shots were fired, the Civil War remains one of the key events in U. S. history. The enormous loss of life alone makes it tragically unique: More Americans died in Civil War battles than in all other American wars combined. More Americans fell at the Battle of Gettysburg than during any battle in American military history. And, in one day at the Battle of Antietam, more Americans were killed and wounded than in any other day in American history.

Slaves did the backbreaking work on Southern plantations.

As tragic as the loss of life was, however, it is the principles over which the war was fought that make it uniquely American. Those beliefs—equality and freedom—are the foundation of American democracy, our basic rights. It was the bitter disagreement about the exact nature of those rights that drove our nation to its bloodiest war.

The disagreements grew in part from the differing economies of the North and South. The warm climate and wide-open areas of the Southern states were ideal for an economy based on agriculture. In the first half of the 19th century, the main cash crop was cotton, grown on large farms called plantations. Slaves, who were brought to the United States from Africa, were forced to do the backbreaking work of planting and harvesting cotton. They also provided the other labor necessary to keep plantations running. Slaves were bought and sold like property, and had been critical to the Southern economy since the first Africans came to America in 1619.

The suffering of African Americans under slavery is one of the great tragedies in American history. And the debate over

whether the United States government had the right to forbid
slavery—in both Southern states and in new territories—was
a dispute that overshadowed the first 80 years of our history.

For many Northerners, the question of slavery was one of
morality and not economics. Because the Northern economy
was based on manufacturing rather than agriculture, there was
little need for slave labor. The primary economic need of
Northern states was a protective tax known as a tariff that
would make imported goods more expensive than goods
made in the North. Tariffs forced Southerners to buy Northern
goods and made them economically dependent on the North,
a fact that led to deep resentment among Southerners.

Economic control did not matter to the anti-slavery
Northerners known as abolitionists. Their conflict with the
South was over slavery. The idea that the federal government
could outlaw slavery was perfectly reasonable. After all,
abolitionists contended, our nation was founded on the idea
that all people are created equal. How could slavery exist in
such a country?

For the Southern states that joined the Confederacy, the
freedom from unfair taxation and the right to make their

**United States in 1861**

| 1 | Confederate States with order of secession |
| States loyal to the Union |
| U.S. territories |

B

\*\*\*\*\*\*\*\*\*6918

02/28/2

2  12:06PM

Ulysses S. Grant /

jnfb

3330501733984117

Expires 03/10/22

Thu

own decisions about slavery was as important a principle as equality. For most Southerners, the right of states to decide what is best for its citizens was the most important principle guaranteed in the Constitution.

The conflict over these principles generated sparks throughout the decades leading up to the Civil War. The importance of keeping an equal number of slave and free states in the Union became critical to Southern lawmakers in Congress in those years. In 1820, when Maine and Missouri sought admission to the Union, the question was settled by the Missouri Compromise: Maine was admitted as a free state, Missouri as a slave state, thus maintaining a balance in Congress. The compromise stated that all future territories north of the southern boundary of Missouri would enter the Union as free states, those south of it would be slave states.

In 1854, however, the Kansas-Nebraska Act set the stage for the Civil War. That act repealed the Missouri Compromise and by declaring that the question of slavery should be decided by residents of the territory, set off a rush of pro- and anti-slavery settlers to the new land. Violence between the two sides began almost immediately and soon "Bleeding Kansas" became a tragic chapter in our nation's story.

With Lincoln's election on an anti-slavery platform in 1860, the disagreement over the power of the federal government reached its breaking point. In early 1861, South Carolina became the first state to secede from the Union, followed by Mississippi, Florida, Alabama, Georgia, Louisiana, Virginia, Texas, North Carolina, Tennessee, and Arkansas. Those eleven states became the Confederate States of America. Confederate troops fired the first shots of the Civil War at Fort Sumter, South Carolina, on April 12, 1861. Those shots began a four-year war in which thousands of Americans—Northerners and Southerners—would give, in President Lincoln's words, "the last full measure of devotion."

OPPOSITE: The Confederate attack on Fort Sumter began the Civil War.

# Introduction:
# "An Acre of Blood"

★ ★ ★ ★ ★

Ulysses Grant rose from a store clerk to a general during the Civil War.

By 1865, the Civil War had dragged on for four terrible years. Despite the bloodshed and brutality, no one on either side really knew when the war would end. President Lincoln and his commander, General Ulysses S. Grant, feared that Southern troops would vanish into the hills and forests of the South and continue fighting for years. Advisers to Confederate leader Robert E. Lee recommended exactly that. They told Lee to order his troops to "scatter like rabbits."

By April, more than 600,000 men from both sides had died. The battles had ranged in size from large-scale conflicts such as Gettysburg to smaller battles, such as the one in Sayler's Creek, Virginia. There, in the days before the end of the war, Union and Confederate troops fought in vicious hand-to-hand combat with bayonets and musket butts. Before the skirmish ended, the troops had been forced to fight with bare hands, biting, clawing, and choking their enemies in a fury. Nearly 10,000 men were killed or wounded on both sides. One of Confederate

General Robert E. Lee's sons was taken prisoner. An observer wrote, "An acre of blood still separates us."

A week after Sayler's Creek, with the Confederate capital of Richmond in flames, Lee finally surrendered to Grant. The stately Southerner arrived at Appomattox Court House in his dress uniform, surrounded by his officers, as Grant—the rumpled, cigar-smoking Union commander—pulled up to join him. Many wondered what the terms of this "unconditional" surrender would be. Few expected mercy. Grant was known as (among other things) the "butcher" of Cold Harbor—he had lost 7,000 men in a half hour assault there, then left his wounded to die in the muck and blood rather than call a truce to save them.

Grant, however, had seen enough horror. Like Lincoln, he had no desire for revenge. Grant took no prisoners and made no harsh demands. Instead, he set Lee and his officers free and allowed any Confederate who owned a horse to take it home so fields could be plowed for planting.

After accepting Lee's sword of surrender, Grant was angered by the sounds of his men shooting cannons and muskets in celebration. He ordered his officers to have the firing stopped and to show greater respect for the defeated army. "The war is over," Grant said, "the Rebels are our countrymen again, and the best sign of rejoicing . . . will be to abstain from all demonstrations in the field."

With those words, the general, who began the war as a store clerk, helped to begin the healing of the worst bloodshed in American history.

9

# Chapter 1

Historians and biographers often like to search the early lives and careers of famous individuals to find hints to future greatness. The first forty years in the life of Ulysses S. Grant, however, provide little evidence that he would eventually become one of America's most celebrated and honored military leaders.

Born in Point Pleasant, Ohio, on April 27, 1822, Hiram Ulysses Grant grew up in small towns in Ohio and then Illinois. Living on what was then America's rugged Western frontier, his father, Jesse Grant, enjoyed moderate success in

OPPOSITE: Ulysses Grant served as the eighteenth president from 1869 to 1877.

business and served in several local government positions. Hiram, or "Ulyss" as he was often called, did not care for his father's leather business, but he did enjoy working on the family farm, especially caring for the horses. Education was important to Jesse Grant, so he made sure that Ulysses, the eldest, attended village schools and then private schools in other towns.

## On to West Point

In 1839, Ulysses was stunned to learn that his father had written to one of the state's senators, asking him to offer his son one of the state's two appointments to West Point. Ulysses was only seventeen—he had no interest in becoming a cadet or in pursuing a military career. He also disliked the prospect of taking the Academy's entrance exam—he hated the idea of failing. Ulysses surprised himself, however, by not failing. He entered West Point in 1839.

Young Grant had decided to reverse his given names to Ulysses Hiram, but when he arrived at West Point, he found that a clerical error listed him as Ulysses S. Grant. Since his mother's middle name was Simpson, he decided to accept the change rather than fight the Academy's bureaucracy. Throughout his military career, he showed this same willingness to shrug off things he couldn't change.

The United States Military Academy at West Point, New York, as it appeared in the early 1800s.

   In his four years at West Point, Grant did not take an active part in Academy life. He spent much of his time alone, engaged in his favorite hobby—reading historical novels. His academic record was mediocre and he was ranked roughly in the middle of his class, but he was very strong in mathematics and he was considered a "genius" at reading maps. These skills, which Grant shared with other great battle-field leaders, would prove useful in many military situations, such as coordinating and directing the movements of 100,000 soldiers divided into

★
In 1838, the year before Grant entered West Point, John Wilkes Booth, Lincoln's assassin, was born in Baltimore, Maryland.
★

13

# West Point

West Point, New York, is the oldest continuously
occupied military post in the United States. It sits on
a rocky plateau on the western bank of the Hudson
River with a commanding view south toward New
York City. During the American Revolution, when
much of the fighting took place in New York and
New England, the Hudson was a vital supply route.
Thus, control of the river was crucial to both
Americans and the British. In fact, General George
Washington thought West Point was the most
important military position in America and established his headquarters there in 1779. To prevent
British ships from sailing up the Hudson, American
troops built forts there and extended a 150-ton iron
chain across the river.

In the late 1700s, soldiers and legislators agreed to
create an institution devoted to the science of
warfare. President Thomas Jefferson signed legislation
establishing the United States Military Academy in
1802. By the time Ulysses Grant went to West Point
in 1839, the military academy was graduating classes
of between forty and fifty young lieutenants every
year. When the Civil War began, a large number of
West Point graduates were given commands in the
Union Army—or they resigned Union commands to

take commands in the Confederate Army. Among the well-known Civil War figures who graduated from West Point and fought on the Confederate side were Confederate President Jefferson Davis; and Confederate Generals Robert E. Lee, Stonewall Jackson, and Joseph Johnston. Union generals, in addition to Grant, included William Sherman, George Meade, and George Thomas—the "Rock of Chickamauga."

One class that made an especially large contribution to the war was the Class of 1846. Known primarily as the class that included the great Stonewall Jackson, twenty of the fifty-nine graduates in 1846 served as generals in the Civil War, though none rose as high in achievement or respect as Jackson. Amazingly, in every major battle Jackson fought in the Civil War, he faced at least one former classmate, including his former roommate, George Stoneman, who commanded the Union cavalry in the battle in which Jackson was killed. The class included George Pickett, leader of the ill-fated charge at Gettysburg, and George B. McClellan, whom Jackson faced in Virginia and at Antietam.

Every Civil War battle had significance for West Pointers. Of sixty major battles fought in the Civil War, fifty-five had West Point graduates on both sides of the conflict. In the remaining battles, a West Point graduate commanded one side or the other.

Julia Dent was the sister of one of Grant's West Point classmates.

corps, divisions, regiments, brigades, and companies. Grant also excelled in horsemanship. He set a West Point high-jump record that stood for many years.

Although he had been sure that he would flunk out of West Point, Grant managed to complete his four years. In 1843, he received a commission as a second lieutenant of infantry. He had applied for, and was turned down by, both the cavalry and the elite engineering corps. Though he didn't get the position he requested, he was relieved that his years at the Academy were over. Years later, in his memoirs, Grant recalled:

> *I hear men say that their happiest days were at West Point. I never had that experience. The most trying days of my life were those that I spent there, and I never recall them with pleasure.*

## An Officer in Love

After graduation, Lieutenant Grant was stationed at an infantry post near St. Louis, Missouri. There, he began spending time at the home of a former classmate named Dent. After a number of visits, Grant discovered that he had fallen in love with Dent's sister, Julia. Unfortunately, by this time his army unit had already moved and he was forced to carry on their courtship by mail.

In 1846, two years before his marriage to Julia, Grant's infantry division was ordered to Texas, where border disputes with Mexico soon led to a declaration of war. This conflict was really the outgrowth of the widely held American belief in "Manifest Destiny"—the idea that it was the

General James Longstreet became one of Lee's closest advisors.

nation's clear (or "manifest") destiny to expand westward to the Pacific Ocean. The fact that much of the land was settled by Hispanic peoples and Native American tribes, or that much of it was officially the territory of the Mexico, mattered little to those who accepted the belief.

Grant's military duties, including his service in the War with Mexico, stretched out his courtship with Julia for four years. They were together only once during that period, but they were finally married in August 1848. One of Grant's attendants at the ceremony was a fellow officer, Lieutenant James Longstreet. A few

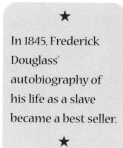

★

In 1845, Frederick Douglass' autobiography of his life as a slave became a best seller.

★

17

The 1840s were a time of rapid expansion across the huge continent.

years later, Longstreet became one of the outstanding generals in the Confederate army and a close assistant to Robert E. Lee.

## Fighting for "Manifest Destiny"

Southern slave owners were strong supporters of Manifest Destiny—and of the war with Mexico. They believed that the survival of their way of life, and of slavery, depended on extending their "peculiar institution" into new western territories. As those territories became ready for statehood, they would balance off new non-slave states and would allow the South to retain equal power with

An illustration
of Grant at the
Battle of
Chapultepec.

Frederick Grant as an adult. As a boy, he stood by his father's side at several battles.

the North in the U.S. Congress. Those who were opposed to the war, like a young Illinois congressman named Abraham Lincoln, soon found that their voices were drowned out.

Though he was ordered to fight in Mexico, Lieutenant Grant also believed the war was "wicked." He called it "one of the most unjust wars ever waged by a stronger against a weaker nation." Despite his personal beliefs, Grant received a citation for action during the American assault on Mexico City. He had taken apart a small howitzer (cannon) in order to carry it up the narrow steps of a steeple. He re-assembled it at the top and, with the advantage of height, successfully destroyed the enemy in the streets below.

★

Julia Dent's parents were slave owners. Grant's parents opposed slavery.

★

The peace treaty that ended the war stripped Mexico of one-third of its territory. The United States received what later became California, New Mexico, Arizona, Utah, Nevada, and parts of Colorado and Wyoming. This was exactly what Americans believed would fulfill their idea of "Manifest Destiny." The addition of these vast western lands, however, added more fuel to a

Ulysses S. Grant

growing conflict over slavery. The debate over whether to allow slavery into the territories made compromise between North and South increasingly difficult.

After their marriage in 1848, Julia and "Ulyss" (as she called him) spent most of the next three years together. In 1851, however, Grant was transferred to the Pacific Coast. The birth of their first child—daughter Nellie—convinced the Grants that the hardship of traveling to the West Coast as a family (part of it overland across Panama) would be too much. Instead, Julia remained on her parents' plantation in Missouri. A second child, Frederick Dent Grant, was born after Grant's departure. The officer did not see his son until he returned to Missouri in 1854.

Grant, who had become a captain, liked the West Coast and considered bringing his family there after he retired from the army. It was after an appointment to a desolate post in California, however, that rumors of a "drinking problem" began to circulate. He was once charged with being "drunk on duty." Although he drank, sometimes a great deal, there was no proof that Grant had an addiction to alcohol. In later years, his critics charged that drinking caused Grant to leave the army in 1854, but he always insisted that he had to resign because he couldn't support his growing family on a captain's pay.

21

# Uncertain Beginnings

★ ★ ★ ★ ★

At the beginning of the Civil War, Ulysses Grant was working for his older brother as a clerk in store owned by their father, earning $800 a year. By 1865, he was one of three men ever to hold the rank of lieutenant general. Grant, however, was not the only military leader who rose from uncertain beginnings to military glory during the Civil War. Three other famous generals who gained fame in the Civil war started slowly.

William Tecumseh Sherman was an unknown forty-one-year-old colonel from Ohio when he fought at the battle of Manassas. Although he fought in General Daniel Tyler's First Division with exceptional courage, he took the defeat badly. Three days later he wrote, "I am sufficiently disgraced now. I suppose I can sneak into some quiet corner." Instead, he went on to become one of the greatest generals in the Civil War and succeeded Grant as the commander of the U.S. Army when Grant was elected president.

Stonewall Jackson resigned from the army in 1850 and took a position as a professor of science and artillery at the Virginia Military Institute. He taught at VMI for ten years and was generally considered one of the worst professors in the school. He was a boring speaker and had no patience for students. In turn, students had little respect for Jackson, calling him such nicknames as "Old Jack" and "Tom Fool." Some drew cartoons of Jackson on the classroom chalkboard, showing a man with enormous feet. Jackson's large shoe size had led to another nickname, "Square Box." When the war broke out in April 1861,

Jackson was assigned to march the VMI cadets to Richmond where they would enlist. He began the war as a lieutenant in charge of volunteers at Harpers Ferry. Within three months, however, he had become the immortal Stonewall Jackson after his stand at the Battle of Bull in Manassas, Virginia.

Robert E. Lee, Grant's adversary at the war's end, is remembered today as perhaps the greatest general on either side during the Civil War. Even Lee, however, got off to a rocky start. At the war's outbreak, he was ordered to organize 40,000 Virginia volunteers. Late in July 1861, Confederate President Jefferson Davis sent Lee into western Virginia where the six western counties refused to accept secession. Lee's assignment was to work with local militia officers to drive out the Union troops. His efforts were a complete and humiliating failure. The officers refused to cooperate with one another, late summer rains destroyed the Confederate timing, and Lee's plan for a surprise attack on Union positions developed so slowly that there was no surprise. Because Lee had not seemed aggressive, the Virginia newspapers labeled him "Granny Lee."

President Davis still had confidence in Lee. Instead of a field command, however, Davis sent Lee to plan defenses for the coastal area of South Carolina, Georgia, and eastern Florida. "This will be," Lee wrote to his daughter Mildred, "another forlorn hope expedition. Worse than western Virginia."

Lee spent the next six months in what seemed like banishment to him. But his posting appeared to help him develop his strategy for waging the war: defend the South by using surprise and swift movement. In March 1862, Lee was called back to Richmond to oversee Confederate military operations, under the "direction" of Jefferson Davis. Thus began his remarkable ascent to greatness.

# Hard Times

Once Grant was out of uniform, he tried to get established in a civilian career. He tried farming land that Julia's parents had given them. The Dents also gave them two slaves, but Grant returned them. Grant's farming career was somewhat doomed from the outset. Before he could farm, he first had to build a house in addition to planting crops. He also had no money to buy livestock.

During the next five years, everything Grant tried turned sour. He lost out in a bid to become a county engineer. He failed as a bill collector. A real estate business with a relative provided only enough income for one partner's family, not two. He began to develop a reputation for hard luck—some people even labeled him a failure. By most accounts, he was a sloppy man with a questionable past and a doubtful future. Julia, however, never lost confidence in her husband. Her support remained vital to him throughout his life.

In 1860, the Grants moved to Galena, Illinois, a bustling frontier town on the Mississippi River. He became a clerk in his father's leather goods store, with his older brother as his boss. Nearly forty years old, Grant must have assumed that this $800 a year job would be his final station in life.

Then came the war. In April 1861, a few weeks after the inauguration of President Abraham

Lincoln, the gray-clad troops of the Confederacy opened fire on Fort Sumter, a Federal installation in Charleston Harbor, South Carolina. This attack plunged America into the Civil War.

Grant, a strong Unionist, was confident that his war experience and West Point training would earn him a commission as a high-ranking officer. Though he disliked uniforms and military bands, he wrote to the Lincoln administration to offer his services. When he received no answer, he went to Cincinnati to seek help from General George McClellan, whom he had known casually at West Point. McClellan was apparently too busy to see him. Once again, it seemed that nothing would go Grant's way. But then his fortune began to change in unexpected ways.

# Chapter 2

## WAR IN THE WEST

**W**hen Grant did not receive a commission to fight in the Civil War, he decided to help in the Illinois governor's recruiting office. He continued to write letters, however, hoping his luck would change. And then it did change—rapidly. First, a group of volunteers—the 21st Illinois Regiment of Infantry—refused to go into service with the man who was their commander, a colonel. Instead, they asked if they could be led by Captain Grant. The governor promoted Grant to "colonel of volunteers" and turned the regiment—the "worst in Illinois"—over to him.

OPPOSITE: Union gunboats bombard Fort Henry on the Tennessee River.

In a matter of weeks, Colonel Grant put his men through a tough training program. Some of the young men complained about the hard work, but they emerged feeling that they were part of a solid, disciplined outfit. They were filled with confidence and eager for combat.

A few weeks later, in August 1861, Grant had another stroke of luck. Congress voted him the rank of brigadier general. Like many early appointments, this one was recommended by a local congressman, Elihu Washburne. Washburne hardly knew Grant, but he wanted to be sure that Illinois received its share of high-ranking officers. The congressman remained a steady supporter of Grant throughout the war.

By early November, having risen from civilian to brigadier general in a few months, Grant was given his first command. He had orders to lead his 3,000 men into Missouri to counter moves by the Confederates in that border state. Grant made use of navy gunboats and steamboats to move his force down the Mississippi to the town of Belmont, Missouri. After brief fighting there and at Paducah, the Federals were forced to withdraw. The battle had little impact on the war, but it did give Grant valuable experience in moving troops and in coordinating battle plans with the navy.

Grant moved his regiment back to Cairo, Illinois. He waited there for two months until orders came to move against two key Rebel forts: Fort Henry on the Tennessee River and Fort Donelson on the Cumberland. The two forts, only about a dozen miles apart, formed the major Confederate defensive line protecting the approach to both Kentucky and Tennessee from the North.

For several months, the mood in the North had been one of gloom, disappointment, and uncertainty. Federal forces had not won the quick victory over Southern troops that most Northerners had expected. In most cases, it was the Rebels who were winning battles and gaining confidence.

Once again, Grant made use of navy steamboats and gunboats to move from Cairo, this time with 15,000 men. As this force approached Fort Henry, the Confederate commander, General Lloyd Tiligham, sent most of his men to Fort Donelson. He remained at Fort Henry with only 100 men— just enough to operate the fort's cannons. On February 6, 1862, the Union's gunboats and armed steamboats engaged in an artillery duel with the fort. They soon knocked out the Fort Henry guns and Tiligham was forced to surrender. When Grant and his men arrived—having disembarked farther up river—the fight was already over.

The next day, Grant led his men overland toward Fort Donelson. By February 11, more Federal troops had arrived, bringing the Union

29

Rebels and Federals battled for several days at Fort Donelson.

strength to about 40,000 men. Grant positioned the troops on hills encircling the fort, while the naval gunboats moved into position on the Cumberland River.

Federal land and naval forces bombarded the fort for several days, but the 20,000 defenders refused to give in. On February 15, 1862, a strong Rebel force tried to break through the Yankee lines and nearly succeeded. Grant's division commanders rushed more troops to close the gap, forcing the Confederates back into the fort.

The next day, the fort's commander, General Simon Bolivar Buckner, asked for the terms of surrender. In a terse statement that instantly became famous, Grant replied that, "No terms except unconditional and immediate surrender can be accepted. I propose to move immediately upon your works."

Buckner was furious. No one had ever heard of such terms before—Grant and Buckner had even been friends before the war. Out of options, Buckner knew he had no choice but to accept. He surrendered Fort Donelson and about 15,000 men.

On February 20, 1862, Abraham Lincoln's son, Willie, 11, died from typhoid fever.

Within hours of the surrender, telegraph wires throughout the country hummed with news of the capture of Forts Henry and Donelson. After nearly a full year of war, the Union finally had a victory. Grant became the first national hero of the war. His picture appeared on the cover of a national magazine. Northern newspapers declared that his initials should now stand for "Unconditional Surrender" Grant. Congress showed its appreciation by promoting him to Major General of Volunteers.

The losses at Forts Henry and Donelson were a serious blow to the South. Until that point, the Confederates had built a firm defensive line from Virginia to Missouri. Grant's triumph had shattered that line. Union forces now controlled both the Cumberland and Tennessee Rivers, giving them a safe invasion route into the South.

31

Tennessee, a Rebel state, and Kentucky, a border state, could no longer be controlled by the South.

One result of the battle for Fort Donelson went largely unnoticed: during the tense days of fighting, General Grant began smoking cigars—not the occasional cigar, but one after another, often twenty or more a day. Later in life, this unhealthy practice would take a serious toll.

## A Costly Surprise at Shiloh

After leading Federal troops in a single major battle, Ulysses S. Grant had gained success and recognition far greater than he could have

In 1862, Pittsburgh Landing on the Tennessee River was the scene of the bloody Battle of Shiloh.

imagined. He must have been pleased by the praise he received, but he also knew how fleeting fame could be. Having seen other officers fail, Grant was well aware that military reputations could be destroyed as rapidly as they were created.

Early in March 1862, the commander of Union armies—General Henry W. Halleck—organized a navy and army expedition to establish a Federal base at Pittsburg Landing, Tennessee, near the Mississippi-Tennessee border. The commander of the expedition was Major General Grant. The general camped his army of 40,000 men in the

33

Union General
Don Carlos Buell

woods and fields surrounding Shiloh Church. He was to wait there for General Don Carlos Buell to arrive with an additional 30,000 Federals.

About twenty miles away, Rebel General Albert Sidney Johnston, commander in chief of Confederate armies in the West, was preparing 40,000 troops to attack. When he learned of the Union troop movements, Johnston concluded that he had to hit Grant's army before Buell's troops arrived.

On April 3, 1862, Johnston put his army on the move. Two nights later, the Rebels were less than a mile from the Federal camp. During that night his officers pleaded with Johnston to withdraw. They were convinced that the Yankees must know they were there and soon would be "entrenched up to their eyes." Johnston was firm. "I would fight them if they were a million," he replied.

The next morning, April 6, Grant's troops were sitting outside their tents at breakfast, while 40,000 Rebels edged closer and closer through the underbrush. Grant had decided not to fortify the camp. He said later that he had wanted his men doing combat drills, not digging trenches.

Ulysses S. Grant

Union riflemen held their ground at the "Hornet's Nest."

At 5:15 A.M., a Union patrol ran into Confederate skirmishers. An officer ran back to Grant's camp. "The Rebels are out there, thicker than fleas on a dog's back!" he shouted.

It wasn't until 9:00 A.M. that the Union blues managed to form a defensive line, stretching from the Shiloh church along a sunken wagon road. From the sunken road, the Yankee shots buzzed through the high grass, leading the men on both sides to call that area the "Hornets' Nest." In their headlong charge, the Southerners couldn't see the

35

General Beauregard
orders Confederate
troops to withdraw
at Shiloh.

sunken road until it was too late and one advancing line after another was cut down.

Grant galloped from place to place, trying to steady the men and to form a second line. In the afternoon, after a brief lull, General Johnston led another assault that nearly broke the Union line. But then Johnston was hit, the bullet severing an artery in his knee. With no medical help nearby, and no one who knew how to tie a tourniquet, he rapidly bled to death.

Another Confederate general, Daniel Ruggles, tried a new tactic. He ordered sixty-two cannons to be moved into position. From there, he unleashed the largest artillery bombardment yet seen in North America. The hail of shells ripped great holes in the Federal lines. Some of the men tried to escape to Pittsburg Landing, but many of them were intercepted and captured. Another 2,800 dead lay in the bottom of the Hornets' Nest—more than half the Federals who had fought there.

Grant tried frantically to establish a new defensive line around the landing. His men were frightened and confused, but Grant was fortunate that the Rebels were too exhausted to take advantage. That night, General Pierre G.T. Beauregard replaced Johnston, confident that victory would be theirs in the morning. The surprise attack had forced Grant's army back two miles and inflicted the heaviest casualties

> ★
> Confederate General P.T. Beauregard had commanded the victorious Rebel troops at Manassas.
> ★

37

of the war so far. The general found thousands of his men cowering on the banks of the Tennessee River, "frantic with fright and utterly demoralized."

Fortune smiled on Grant's battered army that night, as Buell's army arrived on the opposite bank of the Tennessee River. By dawn, however, about 20,000 men had been ferried across the river.

As the morning sun rose, Grant issued a simple order: "Advance and recapture our original camps."

People in the North were stunned by news of the bloody two-day battle. The Union had suffered 13,047 casualties (killed, wounded, and missing), and the South, 10,694. This toll made Shiloh the costliest battle in the nation's history up to that point. In fact, the casualty total at Shiloh was greater than all American losses in the American Revolution, the War of 1812, and the War with Mexico combined.

Grant was severely criticized for allowing his army to be caught by surprise. The high casualty count led the newspapers to call Grant a "butcher"—the same newspapers that were so full of praise for him only a few weeks earlier. Some Ohio newspapers now claimed that Grant had not been born in the state. Despite calls for Grant's removal from command, President Lincoln stood by him. "I can't spare this man," he said simply. "He fights."

Ulysses S. Grant

As fast as Grant's star had risen, it fell twice as fast. General Halleck, Grant's superior, seemed intent on using the embarrassment of Shiloh to humble Grant further. First, he sent angry memos to Grant, with copies to Washington, accusing him of sending reports late or not sending them at all. Next, Halleck accused him of leaving his army to go to Nashville without informing Halleck, and

General Henry W. Halleck

then made a reference to Grant's alleged drinking problem. "A rumor has reached me," he wrote to the president's cabinet, "that General Grant has resumed his former bad habits."

Grant was shocked and bewildered. He knew he was always timely with his dispatches and he took great pride in their accuracy and detail. He could not understand why Halleck had turned against him. Since Grant was such a trusting person, he could not imagine that Halleck's actions were a simple matter of jealousy. His anguish was relieved a few days later when Halleck restored him

★

Throughout the war, Grant suffered from migraine headaches and insomnia.

★

39

During the siege of Vicksburg, Union troops dug a canal across a turn in the Mississippi.

to command, probably because he saw that Lincoln intended to stand by the hero of Fort Donelson. To shift the blame, Halleck lamely explained that an incompetent telegraph operator had misdirected Grant's dispatches.

## Triumph at Vicksburg

General Grant had been restored to his command, but he knew his reputation would be marred until he proved that he deserved the fame he had won at Fort Donelson. While he waited for that opportunity, the nation's attention shifted to the East,

Ulysses S. Grant

where the Union Army of the Potomac searched for a way to reach the Confederate capital of Richmond, Virginia. General Robert E. Lee had been placed in command of the army defending the Confederate capital. He reorganized the troops, named it the Army of Northern Virginia, and then won a series of dazzling victories over the Army of the Potomac. In September 1862, his men bursting with confidence, Lee decided to carry the war into Northern territory by invading Maryland. The Rebel drive was stopped at the bloody Battle of Antietam, and Lee withdrew to Virginia. Later in the year, however, in December, when the Army of the Potomac once again tried to smash through to Richmond, Lee achieved a brilliant victory at the Battle of Fredericksburg.

More Americans died in the one-day Battle of Antietam than in any other day in U.S. history.

In late October, soon after Antietam, Grant was ordered to lead an assault on the city of Vicksburg, Mississippi. Vicksburg was located on high bluffs on the eastern bank of the Mississippi River. It was now the South's main stronghold on the river. In the previous months, Union forces had taken control of most of this vital waterway in both the northern and southern regions, but the Rebels still held a 250-mile stretch of the Mississippi, anchored by Vicksburg. If Union forces could gain control of this stronghold, only a small outpost—Port Hudson—would prevent

41

# The Big Guns

Advances in power and accuracy made the big guns of the Civil War—the artillery—fearsome weapons for both sides. Nowhere were big guns more intimidating than during the siege of Vicksburg.

In the decade before the Civil War, the technique of rifling—cutting grooves inside the barrel of an artillery piece to spin the projectile as it was fired—allowed artillery to shoot farther with greater accuracy than ever before. Artillery, then as now, is divided into three main categories:

**Guns**, also called cannons, use large powder charges to fire in a relatively flat arc. Civil War cannons were named for the weight of the shot they fired. The most widely used cannons were six-, twelve-, and twenty-four pound guns.

**Howitzers** fire shot or shells with a higher elevation. A standard howitzer could fire a shell more than half a mile.

**Mortars** fire heavy projectiles in a high arc. When mortar shells exploded, fragments weighing as much as ten or twenty pounds destroyed anyone or anything within a wide area.

Federals used howitzers on land and mounted on gunboats during the siege of Vicksburg. Perhaps the most famous artillery piece used during the battle, however, was a Confederate howitzer nicknamed "Whistling Dick," which was originally a smooth-bore weapon. When the war broke out, Confederate gunsmiths rifled its barrel. The grooves cut into the barrel were not precise. This flaw gave shells it fired a slight wobble, which in turn produced an eerie whistling sound with each shot. "Whistling Dick" was part of Vicksburg's river defenses and is credited with sinking the Federal gunboat *Cincinnati* during the siege.

them from controlling the entire length of the Mississippi. With the river in Yankee hands, the Confederacy would be cut in two. The western states of Arkansas, Louisiana, and Texas would be isolated from the other eight states, depriving the South of desperately needed food, supplies, and manpower.

Grant welcomed the challenge and opportunity that Vicksburg presented. This was his chance to redeem himself and to restore himself to hero status. He was keenly aware that President Lincoln and members of his cabinet were observing his every move, and he knew they were particularly sensitive to rumors about his drinking. For on-the-spot observation, Secretary of War Edwin Stanton sent his assistant, Charles A. Dana, to stay at Grant's headquarters and send back regular reports.

The men on Grant's staff, and the general himself, knew that Dana's real purpose was to report on Grant's use of alcohol. They urged him to treat Dana as an intruder, cooperating as little as possible. Grant did just the opposite and made the army's camp and headquarters open to the former journalist. To everyone's surprise, Dana's dispatches were filled with praise. In later years, he recalled that:

> *General Grant was the most modest, the most disin-*
> *terested, and the most honest man I ever knew, with a*

43

*temper that nothing could disturb. Not a great man
except morally; not an original or brilliant man, but
sincere, thoughtful, deep, and gifted with courage.*

Within days of receiving the order to attack
Vicksburg, Grant had devised his plan of attack.
He knew that the Rebels had transformed the city
into a small fortress. Along the high bluffs above
the Mississippi, Southern engineers had placed
more than 100 cannons, each protected by strong
log barricades. An attempt by the Federal navy to
bombard the city into submission the previous
year had failed completely. On the landward side,
the city was protected by dense thickets, swamps,
and bayous that extended for miles to the north
and south. The only possible approach to the city
was directly from the east.

Grant first tried a two-pronged attack. With half
his army, he moved south from Memphis, planning
to turn west to attack the city. At the same time, his
most-trusted field commander—General William
Tecumseh Sherman—would move south on the
Mississippi, landing north of Vicksburg. While the
defenders focused on Grant's troops, Sherman's
men would attack from the northeast. The plan was
sound, but Confederate forces detected Grant's first
movement. Rebel General Earl Van Dorn led his
cavalry division completely around Grant's army
and attacked his supply base at Holly Springs,
capturing the defenders and putting mountains of

supplies to the torch. Without supplies, Grant was forced to turn back. Sherman tried to proceed with his part of the plan, but was badly beaten by a Confederate force about five miles from Vicksburg.

While the defenders of Vicksburg and their new commander, General John C. Pemberton, congratulated themselves on their success, Grant once again felt the sting of criticism. One assault came in a letter written by General Cadwallader Washburn to his brother Elihu, Grant's supporter in Congress:

> Grant has no plans for taking Vicksburg. He is frittering away time and strength to no purpose. The truth must be told even if it hurts. You cannot make a silk purse out of a sow's ear.

This most recent setback seemed to make Grant even more determined to grab the prize that was Vicksburg. During the next three months, he had his men dig canals from one river or bayou to another in an effort to get his army below Vicksburg without having to face the wall of cannons on the bluff. But the work crews could not make a canal deep enough, and they were constantly hampered by the swamps, thickets, and muck surrounding the mighty river. Grant needed another plan.

Whenever he was feeling defeated or dead-ended, Grant always received a lift from having Julia with him. Her presence made him feel

whole, confident, and complete. He sent for her and requested that she stay at his headquarters at Milliken's Bend on the Mississippi, about thirty miles north of Vicksburg. Their oldest son, Frederick, also came along. Frederick spent the rest of the Vicksburg campaign with his father, standing proudly in a uniform.

By early April 1863, Grant had devised an inventive, complicated plan for getting his army in position to attack Vicksburg from the east. He worked out the plan with naval commander

Grant's men dug canals from one bayou to the next in a futile attempt to get below Vicksburg.

Admiral David W. Porter, who would sail transport barges and gunboats to a point thirty miles south of Vicksburg. While Porter sailed south, Grant would march an army of 30,000 down the western (Louisiana) side of the Mississippi and meet up with Porter's fleet. The navy would then ferry the men across the mile-wide river to the eastern bank. It was a bold scheme, and a risky one. Porter's armed steamboats and gunboats, with transport barges protected by hay bales strapped to the sides, would have to go as

47

★

In the spring of 1863, while Grant was moving across Mississippi, Robert E. Lee's Rebel army was moving north into Pennsylvania.

★

fast as possible past the blazing artillery fire from Vicksburg. Once they got south of the city, the fleet would have to stay there. Returning upstream against the current would be so slow that the Rebels would blast the boats out of the water.

On the night of April 16, 1863, while Grant, his staff, Julia, and Frederick watched from a steamboat upstream, Porter's boats and transports "ran the gauntlet" of artillery fire and flaming rafts past the city. Only one steamboat was lost. Six days later, as Grant's troops marched south along the west bank, another flotilla challenged the cannons and made it through with only light losses.

By the end of April 1863, Grant and his army had been transported across the Mississippi. Grant's plan so far was working, but it was dangerous. The 30,000-man force was now cut off from its supply base and they were in enemy territory. Each man had rations for only a few days. Troops were told to live off the land in order to supplement the food supply.

The Rebel troops in the region outnumbered Grant's army, but they were widely scattered. Pemberton had about 32,000 men in Vicksburg, another 6,000 were fifty miles east of the city at Jackson, the state capital, and smaller units were at several other outposts. Grant decided to strike each of the separate Confederate forces as quickly as possible before they could combine against him. He also had a cavalry division galloping throughout the countryside, severing communications and creating confusion.

On May 1, 1863, Grant's army encountered about 5,000 Confederate troops at Port Gibson and defeated them after a stubborn, day-long battle. Beating the Rebel force had an almost magical effect on Grant's men. After months of frustration, defeats, canal digging, and waiting, they were thrilled to be on the move again. The men also noticed a new confidence in their commander. They had been uncertain of him at first, partly because he wasn't like other high-ranking officers. His uniform was always dusty and ill-fitting; he wore a floppy hat and a plain coat with little to indicate his rank. He had none of the dash or flair of other generals, and he was not one to give inspiring speeches.

Though he lacked the elite trappings of leadership, Grant was learning how to command. Each new experience, the failures as well as the successes, were molding him into a skilled, confident leader, and his men responded to that. One biographer, Geoffrey Perret, describes Grant's development:

> By 1863, [the men] had come to appreciate his quiet, undemonstrative presence, the lack of show around him and his staff, which was itself singular and striking.

★

On May 2, 1863, Confederate General Stonewall Jackson was mistakenly shot by his men at the Battle of Chancellorsville.

★

49

*Grant felt completely at home with his men, and they*
*with him. . . . During a battle, Grant rode from regiment*
*to regiment in the thick of the fight instead of trying to*
*direct his army from a tent safe in the rear. The troops*
*called him "the Old Man," as if they knew him, yet*
*chances are most would not know him if they met him.*

★
One thing that sent
Grant into a rage
was cruelty to
animals.
★

After the Battle of Port Gibson, Grant
rapidly moved his army to the northeast,
not directly toward Vicksburg. While
Confederate General Pemberton tried to
figure out where Grant was, where he was
headed, and how many men he had, Grant
did all he could to keep the Rebel
commander puzzled. Grant ordered Sherman to
march from Milliken's Bend toward Jackson, while
Grant's force defeated another Rebel outpost on
May 12. Two days later, Sherman's troops arrived
and were sent into Jackson, where they destroyed
warehouses and railroad facilities and forced the
6,000 defenders to leave.

Pemberton could finally see what Grant was up
to, but it was too late. He sent a frantic telegram
to Confederate President Jefferson Davis in
Richmond, reporting that "Grant threatens
Jackson and, if successful, cuts off Vicksburg and
Port Hudson from the East."

As Grant's army turned west toward Vicksburg,
Pemberton moved out to meet him with a force of
about 23,000 men. The two armies collided at a

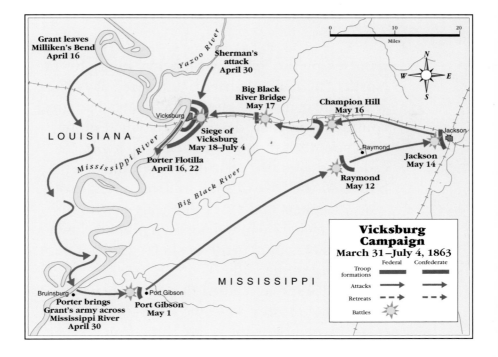

Map labels:

Grant leaves Milliken's Bend April 16

Yazoo River

Sherman's attack April 30

Big Black River Bridge May 17

Champion Hill May 16

Jackson

LOUISIANA

Vicksburg

Siege of Vicksburg May 18–July 4

Mississippi River

Porter Flotilla April 16, 22

Big Black River

Raymond

Jackson May 14

Raymond May 12

MISSISSIPPI

Bruinsburg

Port Gibson

Porter brings Grant's army across Mississippi River April 30

Port Gibson May 1

0 10 20 Miles

N W E S

**Vicksburg Campaign**
March 31–July 4, 1863

| | Federal | Confederate |
|---|---|---|
| Troop formations | ▬▬ | ▬▬ |
| Attacks | → | → |
| Retreats | --→ | --→ |
| Battles | ✳ | ✳ |

place called Champion's Hill on May 16. After a battle that a Union officer called, "one of the most obstinate and murderous conflicts of the war," the Confederates were forced to retreat.

Grant's movements with his army had been remarkable. In seventeen days, his men had marched 180 miles, fought and won five separate battles, and had now trapped Pemberton's 30,000 troops inside Vicksburg.

The Union troops were filled with confidence as they began digging trenches and setting up artillery to close an iron ring around Vicksburg. Like their commander, they wanted to attack the city while they had the momentum. Grant ordered an assault on May 19 that was easily repulsed by the Rebels with heavy losses for the North. The Federals tried again three days later, with similar results. The Confederates had great confidence in their defenses. They had more than seventy cannons, protected by log barricades and rifle pits, glaring down from steep bluffs. At the base of each hill was a tangle of thickets and vines that trapped the attackers while defenders poured down a steel wall of artillery shells, canister shot, and minié balls.

As the Civil War claimed more lives in the South, some Confederate leaders proposed arming the slaves to fight the Union.

Grant concluded that the only way to take the city was by a siege—he would prevent anyone or anything from getting into or out of Vicksburg. Pemberton and his men were confident they could hold out until the Confederate high command sent a relief army to raise the siege.

The siege dragged on, however, day after day, week after week, and the spirits of the defenders and of the 3,500 civilians trapped in the city began to decline. In one of the rare messages to make it past the Union lines, Pemberton asked, "Am I to expect reinforcements? From what direction and how soon?"

Meantime, the siege dragged on, punctuated by constant artillery fire from Grant's army. A Vicksburg civilian later wrote, "Hardly any part of the city was outside the range of the enemy's artillery . . . . Just across the Mississippi . . .

mortars were put in position and trained directly on the homes of the people."

After seven weeks, the Confederate troops were too weak from hunger to fight, and Pemberton knew it was time to surrender. On July 3, 1863, he heard Grant's terms: "You will be allowed to march out, the officers taking with them their side arms and clothing, and the field, staff, and cavalry officers one horse each. The rank and file will be allowed all their clothing but no other property."

Union artillery fired more than 2,500 shells a day into Vicksburg.

The next day, July 4—Independence Day— the exhausted, ragged defenders of Vicksburg marched out of their defenses, stacked their weapons, and signed their paroles—agreements not to take up arms again. The Union troops displayed respect and courtesy for the defeated Rebels, and many shared their rations with the gaunt defenders. In his *Memoirs*, Grant noted, "When they passed out of the works they had so long and gallantly defended . . . not a cheer went up, not a remark was made that would give pain."

The loss of Vicksburg was a severe blow to the Confederacy. In addition to the 30,000 men who surrendered, the battles had resulted in more than 10,000 casualties. These were veteran fighters that the South, with its limited population, could not replace. The defenders also gave up 172 cannons and 60,000 small arms.

Union admiral David Porter ran his ships under a barrage from Confederate guns at Vicksburg.

Defeat at Vicksburg was only one-half of the devastating Independence Day news for the Confederacy. At exactly the same time, July 1 to 3, 1863, Federal forces defeated General Robert E. Lee's army at the Battle of Gettysburg in Pennsylvania. The two losses represented the turning point of the war. A few days later, Confederate forces at Port Hudson surrendered, giving the North control of the entire length of the Mississippi and dividing the Confederacy in two. The Confederates were on the defensive and their only hope was that war-weariness might eventually lead the North to seek peace.

Grant's personal reputation once again soared.

54

The press, the Northern public, and government leaders could not find enough words to describe his greatness. President Lincoln, who had thought Grant was headed for disaster when he led his army across the Mississippi, wrote a letter of apology and praise to his general. "I now wish to make the personal acknowledgement that you were right and I was wrong," Lincoln wrote. "I write this now as a grateful acknowledgement for the almost inestimable service you have done this country."

## Emancipation

President Lincoln's Emancipation Proclamation, which had taken effect on January 1, 1863, declared that all slaves in the states still at war with the Union were free. Critics of Lincoln's policy were quick to point out that no slaves were actually freed by the statement, since all eleven states in the Confederacy were still in a "state of rebellion," and the proclamation did not apply to slave states—known as border states—that had remained in the Union. No slaves would actually be freed until the Union armies set them free.

The proclamation was actually more effective than the critics realized. The African American "grapevine," which spread news throughout the South, rapidly informed slaves everywhere of the government policy. The proclamation also put an end to Southern plans for arming the slaves.

55

After January 1, hundreds and then thousands of slaves simply walked off their plantations, or ran away if the owners had not fled, as soon as they heard that a Federal army was approaching. Instead of using the old "Underground Railroad" to the North or Canada, they now headed for the nearest Union army camp.

This situation put General Grant and his officers in a unique position. Grant's Army of the Tennessee had its headquarters at Milliken's Bend on the Mississippi River, and many freed slaves headed there. Others followed Grant's army as the troops raced through Mississippi toward Vicksburg— including the slaves from the plantation of Jefferson Davis, president of the Confederacy.

While this outbreak of freedom was exciting at first, the former slaves soon found they had been cut adrift. They were wandering in a world they did not really understand. While many Federal officers welcomed them, others did not. Some were even willing to return freed slaves to their former owners.

Grant established a refugee camp at Grand Junction, Tennessee, and persuaded a chaplain named John Eaton to manage it. The former slaves were put to work, either in the camp or on projects, such as repairing railroads and bridges, or picking cotton and other crops from abandoned plantations. They were now paid for their labor

Ulysses S. Grant

instead of being forced to work. They also received regular rations, medical care, and shelter, as well as protection from former owners. By mid-1863, the Grand Junction camp was so crowded that Grant was forced to turn people away.

Grant also had volunteer officers begin military training for any of the young men who wanted to be in the Union army. These men began their training in the spring of 1863 at about the same time that African Americans in the East were forming the famed 54th Massachusetts Regiment. In June 1863, several hundred of Grant's recruits were training with white officers at Milliken's Bend, about thirty miles north of Vicksburg, when the base was attacked by a Rebel force. The surprise attack hurled the Federals back toward the river. With their backs to the Mississippi, the Union troops, white and black, held their own until Union gunboats arrived to drive off the attacking force.

★

Two of Frederick Douglass' sons served in the 54th Massachusetts Regiment.

★

After the action, a Union officer praised the African American recruits for standing firm in what he called "one of the fiercest battles I have seen." And a Confederate general said the freedmen faced a Rebel charge with "considerable obstinacy, while the white—or true—Yankee portion ran like whipped curs."

President Lincoln was pleased and thankful for Grant's efforts on behalf of the former slaves. In a

Freed African Americans left the South to enlist in the Union forces.

letter that was printed in many newspapers, he praised Grant but avoided mentioning him by name, perhaps because many people still opposed the policy of emancipation:

> Some of the commanders of our armies in the field who have given us our most important successes [i.e. Grant], believe the emancipation policy, and the use of colored troops, constitute the heaviest blow yet dealt to the rebellion.

Lincoln also looked into the future, predicting that African Americans would recall their military service with great pride, while prejudiced whites

Ulysses S. Grant

would continue their opposition to freedom and equality:

> *. . . There will be some black men who can remember that, with silent tongue, and clenched teeth, and steady eye, and well poised bayonet, they have helped mankind to this great consummation [emancipation]; while, I fear, there will be some white ones, unable to forget that, with malignant heart, and deceitful speech, they have strove to hinder it.*

## General Grant to the Rescue

A few weeks after Grant's brilliant victory at Vicksburg, he suffered a painful leg injury in a riding accident when his horse fell on top of him. In October 1863, he was still hobbling painfully when he received word from Washington that he was to leave Vicksburg and go to Chattanooga in Southeastern Tennessee, where a Union army led by General William Rosecrans was in serious trouble. A few weeks earlier, Rosecrans had led his Army of the Cumberland into Tennessee toward Chattanooga. With a well-supplied force of 60,000 men, he was confident he

General Braxton Bragg

59

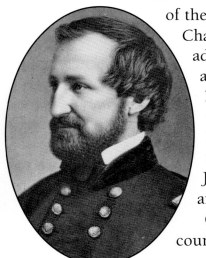

could defeat a Rebel army of 43,000 led by General Braxton Bragg. In the long campaign that followed, both men would be removed from their command. Each general, at different times, had victory within his grasp, but then failed at critical moments.

General Rosecrans was the first to mismanage his opportunity. He encountered Bragg's Rebels on the banks of the Tennessee River near Chattanooga. As the Federals advanced, Bragg retreated, abandoning Chattanooga, and Rosecrans closed in for the victory. He failed to realize that Bragg was drawing him into a trap while waiting for General James Longstreet to arrive with another 20,000 men.

On September 18, 1863, Bragg counter-attacked and the two armies collided along Chickamauga Creek in one of the bloodiest battles of the war. When Rosecrans made the fatal mistake of pulling one of his regiments out of position, Bragg seized the opportunity. With the fierce Rebel Yell, Bragg's Confederates charged and cut the

TOP: General George Thomas, "The Rock of Chickamauga." BOTTOM: Union General William Rosecrans.

Ulysses S. Grant

Federal force in two. Rosecrans and most of his officers joined thousands of Union blues in a wild retreat. The Union army was saved from complete disaster by General George Thomas who rallied enough men to hold back the Rebels until nightfall before pulling back. For his heroic feat, Thomas became known as the "Rock of Chickamauga."

The Union losses were horrifying— 16,170 dead, wounded, or missing. That was 28 percent of the men involved. The Army of the Cumberland was so battered and disorganized that one final push by Bragg would have totally destroyed what was left. But Bragg's army had also suffered huge losses— more than 18,000 casualties —and he concluded that such a push was impossible. Despite his great victory, Bragg allowed the Union force to retreat into Chattanooga.

The Federal army quickly found itself under siege. Bragg positioned most of his troops on two high areas—Lookout Mountain and Missionary Ridge—with artillery trained on Chattanooga below. Before being cut off by the siege, Union reinforcements had rushed to the town—General Joseph Hooker with 20,000 men. But these added troops soon found that, like the remnants of Rosecrans' army, they were trapped in Chattanooga. There was no way to move an entire army out of the town without being shredded by

Grant and his commanders on Lookout Mountain, Tennessee.

Rebel artillery. To make matters worse, the Confederates closed off every supply route, which quickly brought the Federals close to starvation.

General Grant made his way into Chattanooga on October 23, 1863, about a month into the siege. Even before he arrived, he had removed Rosecrans from command and replaced him with General Thomas. As he surveyed the half-starved men, and the thousands of dead or dying horses and mules, Grant must have been struck at the irony of finding himself inside a city under siege

Ulysses S. Grant

rather than directing a siege from the outside. In his *Memoirs*, he noted that, "It looked, indeed, as if but two courses were open: the one to starve, the other to surrender or be captured."

Grant, however, soon found a third course. He planned to open a water route to the town of Bridgeport, Tennessee. From there, he planned to bring food and ammunition into the besieged town. On his first night in Chattanooga, he recalled, "I issued orders for opening the route to Bridgeport—a 'cracker line' as the soldiers. . . term it." "Cracker" is an insulting term for poor Southern whites.

★
Sherman was given the first name Tecumseh—in honor or the great Shawnee chief—at birth. He took the name William as a young man.
★

Grant waited a month to reorganize his troops and for Sherman to arrive with 16,000 men. General Bragg, meantime, unaware of Grant's plans, remained confident that it was only a matter of time before the Federals would be forced to surrender. Looking down from his hilltop command center, he told a visitor, "There are not enough Yankees in Chattanooga to come up here. They are all my prisoners."

Three days after that boast, Sherman's troops arrived on the other side of the Tennessee River. Grant had Sherman move his men across the river under cover of darkness and climb halfway up Missionary Ridge, then dig in. "We worked like beavers," one of Sherman's men reported. "No spade was idle for a moment. Daylight found us

63

there, two thousand strong, with rifle pits a mile in length. Other brigades [followed]. . . . What a sight for General Bragg when he woke up that morning at his headquarters perch on top of Missionary Ridge!"

On November 19, 1863, President Lincoln delivered his most famous speech: The Gettysburg Address.

On November 24, 1863, Grant ordered an attack on three fronts: Sherman would lead off from the Union's left flank, with Hooker on the right, and Thomas in the center. The assault quickly ran into trouble. First, Sherman's men were stalled by the Confederates and Hooker's men had to stop to repair a bridge destroyed by the

Ulysses S. Grant

The Battle of Lookout Mountain, near Chattanooga, Tennessee.

Southerners. Grant sent word to Thomas to begin the charge up the center of Missionary Ridge, but to stop halfway up.

General Thomas gave the order and 25,000 men started up the steep hillside. These were the men who had been humiliated at Chickamauga, and they wanted glory. They knew they had been ordered to stop halfway up, and Grant was furious when he saw that they didn't even slow down. In one of the most amazing episodes of the entire war, the men surged forward, scrambling over rocks and fallen trees, ignoring the shouts of their officers to stop.

On the crest of Missionary Ridge, the Confederates stared in disbelief as Federals stormed the first trenches and kept coming. The Rebels panicked and began fleeing wildly. A Union soldier later recalled what he saw as he reached the top:

> Gray clad men rushed wildly down the hill and into the woods, tossing away knapsacks, muskets, and blankets as they ran. . . . Officers, frantic with rage, rushed from one panic-stricken group to another, shouting and cursing as they strove to check the headlong flight. . . . In ten minutes all that remained of the defiant Rebel army that had so long besieged Chattanooga was captured guns, disarmed prisoners, moaning wounded, ghastly dead, and scattered demoralized fugitives. Missionary Ridge was ours.

The victory was a great one for Grant. First at Fort Donelson, then Vicksburg, and now Chattanooga—he had fought three major battles against three major armies, winning decisive victories each time. While he had demonstrated his brilliance with his daring moves in the Vicksburg campaign, Chattanooga may have been more remarkable because he first had to restore the morale and organization of an army that had been badly beaten at Chickamauga. He also had to find a way to get food and ammunition to that army—a challenge that had bested all others.

Beneath Grant's sloppy, shy exterior was an inner core of iron will.

Once again, newspapers throughout the North hailed General Grant as the savior of the nation. Congress showed its gratitude by having a special gold medal struck and reviving for him the rank of lieutenant general, a position held previously only by George Washington and Winfield Scott, hero of the War of 1812 and the War with Mexico. Lieutenant General Grant was ordered to Washington, D.C. to receive his new commission and to discuss with President Lincoln plans for ending the war.

Braxton Bragg, who had failed to follow up his great victory at Chickamauga, was removed from command. His friend, President Jefferson Davis, made Bragg his personal military adviser. The defeat at Chattanooga ended any hope the South had of controlling Tennessee, which was now controlled by military governor Andrew Johnson. The Federals could turn their attention south to Georgia, where they had the chance to drive a wedge through the Confederacy all the way to the Atlantic coast.

# Chapter 3

## THE FINAL CAMPAIGN

Lieutenant General Grant, accompanied by his staff and his oldest son, thirteen-year-old Frederick, arrived in Washington in early March 1864. On March 8, Grant was formally presented to the president and his cabinet in the White House. It was the first time Lincoln and Grant had met. Following the meeting, a reception was held in the Blue Room, where the crush of people was so great that Grant was asked to stand on a sofa in order to be seen.

OPPOSITE: General Grant at the front of his troops.

The people who crowded around Grant were not impressed by his appearance. He was shy and often mumbled when he spoke, except when he was giving orders. He wore a plain, wrinkled uniform that fit him poorly, and he wore no medals or other officers' decorations. The short, round-shouldered general was said to be "scared looking." Some observers said he looked like "an awkward hayseed," and one writer said he was like a "stumbling, seedy hick;" the most forgiving comments said he looked "for all the world like a country storekeeper or a western farmer."

The next day, Grant received his commission as lieutenant general, which also made him commander of all Union Armies. In meetings with Lincoln, he explained his plans for the final campaign. In the past, he said, each of the armies had operated independently of the others, "like a balky team" of horses or mules. But now things would be different.

One key part of the plan, and one the president had been urging, was to take advantage of the North's greater manpower. Throughout the country, the Union had about 530,000 men in uniform and listed another 300,000 on its muster rolls. Newspapers called it the greatest army in history. By contrast, the South now had barely 200,000 men in uniform and might have been able to call up another 200,000. Robert E. Lee's Army of Northern Virginia, the largest of the

Confederate forces, numbered barely 60,000. Across the Rapidan River from Lee, General Meade had about 120,000 in the Army of the Potomac.

To make use of this superiority in numbers, Grant planned to strike steadily and relentlessly, especially at Lee's army. There would be no pause after each battle. Instead, the Army of the Potomac would press ahead, giving Lee no room to maneuver and no time to take the initiative. Confederate General James Longstreet, Grant's friend both before and after the war, knew how Grant would operate. "That man," Longstreet said, "will fight us every day and hour till the end of the war."

The one drawback to this plan was that it was likely to lead to increased casualties. It meant one frontal assault after another, rather than careful maneuvering. Grant was keenly aware of this danger, but he felt the strategy would ultimately be justified—he truly believed it would shorten the war. In fact, he was certain this was the only way to force the South to surrender. In his memoirs, Grant explained it this way:

> The losses inflicted, and endured, were destined to be severe; but the armies now confronting each other had already been in deadly conflict for three years, with immense losses. . . and neither had made any real progress toward accomplishing the final end. . . . The

71

*campaign now begun [would] result in heavier losses to both armies, in a given time, than any previously suffered; but the carnage was to be limited to a single year.*

## The End of Gallantry

Before 1864, the press and the public viewed the terrible battles of the Civil War in the light of chivalry and honor, with brave men willing to sacrifice their lives for ideals they believed in deeply. From April 1864 to Lee's surrender a year later, that sense of gallantry was erased by Grant's single-minded determination to destroy the Confederate forces once and for all. Battles that had once been regarded with a certain kind of nobility now became bitter and desperate fights to the death. Place names like Cold Harbor, Petersburg, and Spotsylvania were turned into grisly killing fields.

★

During 1864, more than 200,000 soldiers deserted from the Union army.

★

By the first of May 1864, General Grant had his coordinated armies on the move. Riding along with the marching men of the Army of the Potomac, Grant thought they looked "in splendid condition, [as if] they feel like whipping somebody."

Instead of opposing the crossing, Lee moved his men into a region of northern Virginia called the Wilderness. This was a large area of swampy black muck, jungle-like woods, and thickets where men could see only a few feet in any direction. Grant

Ulysses S. Grant

had hoped he could get past the Wilderness before confronting the enemy. Lee wanted a battle in the Wilderness, where being outnumbered two-to-one was not as much of a disadvantage.

A year earlier, Lee's victory in the same region had encouraged him to invade the North.

On May 5, the Union advance guard encountered part of Lee's army and the Rebels quickly moved off the road into the thickets. A year earlier in nearby Chancellorsville, Lee had won a spectacular victory over the Army of the Potomac in this same tangle of under-growth. As the Federals moved cautiously over the swampy ground, they frequently stepped on half-submerged skulls or other remains of that earlier fight. Men on both sides fired blindly into the thickets, rarely knowing what was in front of them. Union private Warren Goss wrote:

> "It was a blind and bloody hunt to the death . . . [like] two wild animals hunting each other. War had seen nothing like it."
> . . . I stumbled, fell, and my outflung hands pushed up a [pile] of leaves. The fire sprang into flames, caught in the hair and beard of a dead sergeant, and lighted a ghastly face and wide open eyes. I rushed away in horror.

And Private Goss reported that "the men fought the enemy and flames at the same time. Their hair and beards were singed and their faces

73

blistered. . . . Their rifles . . . became so hot . . . that they were unable to hold them." More than 200 wounded Federals were trapped by the flames and never made it out. In a strangely touching sight, Union and Confederate troops worked together during the night to pull men out.

The next morning, as the fighting see-sawed back and forth, Confederate General Longstreet launched a counter-attack that overwhelmed the Union line. As Longstreet moved forward to press the attack with corps commander General Jenkins, they were accidentally fired on by their own men. Jenkins was killed and Longstreet was wounded. Other officers tried to re-organize the attack, but the men were too bewildered by what had happened to press their advantage. The assault was turned back. As darkness fell, the two armies dug in; the battle was a stalemate.

Two days of fighting in what the soldiers called the "Devil's Garden" had resulted in staggering casualties. The Union lost 2,246 killed, 12,037 wounded, and 3,387 missing—17,666 total casualties out of an army of 100,000. The Confederacy had no official figure, but total casualties were considerably lower—about 8,000 men. Still, Lee could ill afford losing so many out of his 60,000-man force.

The next day, May 7, 1864, soldiers on both sides assumed that General Grant, having failed

Ulysses S. Grant

The Wilderness was an area of thick, tangled brush and dense woods.

to defeat Lee, would now "skedaddle," as every general before him had done. But Grant had no intention of retreating. He told a reporter who was on his way to Washington: "If you see the President, tell him for me, that whatever happens, there will be no turning back."

Grant studied the map and concluded that, if he could get his army to a crossroads village called Spotsylvania Court House ahead of the Confederates, he would have his troops positioned between Lee's army and Richmond.

75

Cut off from the capital and supplies, Lee would soon have to surrender.

One of Lee's great strengths, however, was his ability to figure out his enemy's tactics. Although his staff officers were certain Grant would retreat, Lee insisted, "General Grant is not going to retreat. He will move his army to Spotsylvania. . . . I am so sure of his next move that I have already made arrangements to march by the shortest practicable route, so that we may meet him there."

The race was on for the Spotsylvania crossroads. When the Federals arrived, they found the Confederates already there, having arrived just in time to turn and start shooting. The Confederates, it turned out, had a ready-made defense already in place— one of the outer works for the defense of Richmond. The Army of the Potomac found the Rebels firmly entrenched behind seven miles of breastworks made of logs and mud.

A direct assault on those positions looked like pure suicide. And yet Grant had said he would launch direct assaults on Lee's forces whenever he had the chance. In a dispatch to Washington, he wrote: "I am sending back. . . for a fresh supply of provisions and ammunition, and propose to fight it out on this line if it takes all summer."

After two Union probes were pushed back, Grant ordered a predawn attack in fog and rain on a weak point in Lee's line—a salient, or bulge, in the defenses. Fearing that his army would be cut in two, Lee ordered a counter-attack. Both sides then rushed reinforcements into the salient, causing a jam-up of men—and bodies—that led the troops to call this bulge the "Bloody Angle." The two sides engaged in the fiercest hand-to-hand combat of the entire war. Men fought with muskets and bayonets first, then with rifle butts, knives, and fists. This frenzied struggle continued hour after hour as rain turned the battlefield into a quagmire of mud and blood.

The Spotsylvania campaign continued for twelve days, as the usual heavy toll of casualties mounted—17,500 for the Union army, and, for the Confederates, more than 6,000 reported casualties (killed, wounded, and missing) plus about 4,000 captured. Once again, Lee found his fighting strength seriously reduced.

The next collision came at another crossroads village—Cold Harbor—only about ten miles from Richmond. Again, the Confederates were well entrenched, and again Grant ordered a direct assault—at 4:30 A.M. on June 3, 1864. In less than thirty minutes, more than 7,000 Union soldiers were killed or wounded. Never had so many men been sacrificed in such a short time. During a brief truce, a Confederate officer said, "It seemed like murder to fire upon you." Even General Grant, who often seemed oblivious to the high

# The Finest Hour

★ ★ ★ ★ ★

When U.S. Grant is assessed as a military leader, he is often criticized for his battle strategies that resulted in enormous loss of life for troops under his command. Though there is little question that Grant's tactics could not measure up against those of Robert E. Lee, the role played by Grant in bringing the war to an end is often overlooked. Few people realize how close our nation came to a fighting a war that could have lasted for decades.

Even on April 9, the day of Lee's surrender, the Confederates—outnumbered six to one, sick and starving—were not ready to give in. Lee, in fact, planned to send his men on a surprise attack to break though Union lines. Led by General John Gordon, the Rebels would then head for the Blue Ridge Mountains where they could hold out "for twenty years," in one commander's words.

Before dawn that day, the Rebel advance began. As the sun rose, the Rebels attacked, driving back Federal cavalry and capturing several cannons. Reaching the crest of a hill, however, Gordon saw a solid wall of Union soldiers two miles wide advancing toward them. There was no choice but for Lee to surrender. "I would rather die a thousand deaths," said Lee.

At 1:30 P.M on April 9, 1865, a scene took place that instantly became part of American folklore. Lee appeared in a spotless gray uniform, complete with sash and a jewel-studded dress sword. Grant rode in moments later in his well-worn uniform, and half-buttoned private's shirt. At first, he appeared awe-struck in the presence of the great Robert E. Lee. Yet despite his nerves, his ragged appearance, and his reputation as a cigar-chewing "butcher," Grant was about embark on his finest hour and take on his most important task—that of statesman.

Sitting at separate tables, Lee listened as Grant's aide read the most generous terms imaginable. There would be no prison, no parade of captured Confederates down Washington's streets, no charges of treason. Confederate officers could keep their side arms and horses. The men only had to sign a parole agreeing not to fight again.

Lee, shocked by the generosity, thanked Grant, saying, "This will do much toward conciliating our people." Then Lee asked Grant what he could do about the many Union prisoners he held. He could not feed them. "Indeed, I have nothing for my own men," Lee said. Without hesitation, Grant offered to send enough rations for 25,000 across the lines. Was that enough, he wondered? "An abundance, I assure you," replied Lee.

As word spread, men shouted, hugged, and jumped with joy. Grant ordered the celebrations to stop. "The war is over," he said. "The rebels are our countrymen again." As Grant watched Lee ride back to Rebel lines, their eyes met. Grant simply lifted his hat in a sign of respect to the great general. Lee, in return, tipped his own hat. As he rode away, Federal officers along the way followed Grant's example and tipped their hats to Lee. For the dignified loser and the gracious winner, it was the greatest moment of the terrible war.

Federal trenches outside Petersburg, Virginia.

number of casualties, was disturbed by this tragedy. Later he wrote, "I regret this assault more than any one I ever ordered."

As the two armies faced each other across a no-man's land littered with dead and wounded Union soldiers, Grant tried to figure out his next move. After a month of his strategy of direct assaults, Union losses totaled about 50,000—roughly 40 percent of his original army; Rebel losses, estimated at 32,000, amounted to about 46 percent of the South's strength.

Grant began to realize that even the great human resources of the North could not withstand the heavy toll. The public would not stand for it. He began to look for a less costly way. Instead of trying to hammer his way into Richmond, he now directed his army to Petersburg, an important rail center vital to the South's supply line. Instead of a direct attack, Grant was again willing to resort to siege, with the men digging elaborate trench systems to hold the Rebels at bay. A huge supply base was built and a railroad constructed from the James River to the siege lines, providing Union troops with ample food, ammunition, and clothing.

Lee could see clearly that his ragged, half-starved army could not hold out much longer. "Without some increase of our strength," he reported, "I cannot see how we are to escape the natural consequences of the enemy's numerical superiority." As the siege dragged on through the summer of 1864, then into the autumn and winter, Grant had his troops extend the trenches farther and farther to the west, making Lee stretch his men thinner.

Throughout the winter, men on both sides shivered in mud-filled, rat-infested trenches. While the Union troops at least had enough food and clothing, the Rebels were weak with hunger, shoeless, and wearing such rags that it was hard

81

A dead Confederate soldier at Petersburg.

to tell enlisted men from officers. Late in March
1865, some of this tattered, skeletal force made a
desperate attempt at a breakout, but the attack
was easily repulsed.

   Lee's Army of Northern Virginia was no longer
a fighting force and Grant knew it. On April 1,
1865, his cavalry under General Sheridan crushed
the Rebel right wing and took 5,000 prisoners.
The next day, Grant ordered 60,000 men to
advance along a 12-mile front. Somehow a force

Ulysses S. Grant

of 1,000 Confederates held them off for two hours, giving Lee time to move his army.

There was little Lee could do. Sherman's army had powered its way through Georgia and was now moving north, creating a path of destruction sixty miles wide through the Carolinas. Even if Lee could join up with Johnston, their two starved armies would be crushed between Grant and Sherman. And, as Lee led his men along the banks of Appomattox River, Richmond was left unprotected. The officials of the Confederate government fled the city, except for a few who stayed to oversee the torching of the Confederacy's arsenal and warehouses. Soon the whole city was in flames. One eyewitness reported that

> . . . It was as if all the horrors of the final conflagration. . . . The roaring, crackling and hissing of the flames, the bursting of shells at the Confederate Arsenal, the sounds of the instruments of martial music, the neighing of horses, the shouting of the multitude [said] . . . . "The Yankees! The Yankees are coming!

On April 4, 1865, President Lincoln and his son Tad arrived in Richmond where he was cheered by large crowds of Union soldiers and now-free African Americans. Lincoln had been with Grant for several days and was on hand for some of the final combat of the war.

83

Grant and his wife were supposed to accompany the Lincolns to Ford's Theater, but cancelled at the last minute.

★

Lee continued to try to escape with what remained of his army, but he was finally forced to surrender on April 9, 1865, at Appomattox Court House in Virginia. Five days later, on April 14, the nation suffered the final tragedy of the war when Lincoln was mortally wounded by assassin John Wilkes Booth. He died the next day, and Vice President Andrew Johnson was sworn in as President.

## The Grant Legacy

During the Civil War, and in the years since, historians and many others have debated the merits of Ulysses S. Grant as a general. He is frequently compared to his Confederate counterpart, Robert E. Lee—but Lee almost always comes out in a better light. Both men won battles in spectacular fashion; both suffered defeats and made costly mistakes. Many military historians, however, feel that Grant falls short of Lee for two important reasons:

First, Grant critics say, he almost always had superior numbers as well as greater firepower and better weapons, such as repeating rifles. Lee, on the other hand, was usually outnumbered, sometimes with an army half the size of the Union force. Mary Boykin Chestnut, who wrote a fascinating diary of her life in the Confederacy, put the matter simply: "If General Lee had Grant's

Ulysses S. Grant

resources, he would have bagged the last Yankee, or [had] them all safe back in Massachusetts."

The second point the critics make is about temperament—General Grant, they say, used his greater numbers in reckless and ruthless ways. Many of the newspapers of the day called him a "butcher," because he often won by pouring more and more men into a battle until he crushed the enemy. The final drive toward Richmond, starting in the spring of 1864, is a perfect example. In one month of fighting, Grant's army suffered 55,000 killed or wounded in making an advance of only seventy miles. That was more than forty percent of Grant's force. Charles Francis Adams, Jr. who always supported Grant, wrote that the Union army "has literally marched in blood and agony from the Rapidan [River] to the James [River]."

One of the most serious charges against Grant was his decision to attack at Cold Harbor. Not only did he sacrifice 7,000 men in a few minutes of direct assault, he actually tried a total of three assault waves that day. The men in the third wave simply refused to go. Then, during a three-day lull after the battle, he made no move for a truce that would allow him to recover the Union dead and wounded. For three days, the men in the trenches heard the moans and cries of their wounded comrades. But Grant would not call a

★

On his visit to Richmond after it fell, Lincoln stopped at the home of Confederate General George Pickett, a friend before the war.

★

85

truce. According to military tradition, asking for a truce was an admission that you had lost the battle, and Grant had no intention of allowing Lee to claim the victory. As a result of this stubborness, however, hundreds of his men died in terrible agony.

In defense of Grant, he did realize that Cold Harbor was a tragic mistake, one that he admitted and regretted. It was also a mistake from which Grant learned. It was after this disaster that he changed his approach and turned to siege warfare instead of frontal attacks.

Another point in Grant's favor is that he was not even involved in two of the bloodiest battles of the war. The Battle of Antietam in September 1862, was the bloodiest single day of the war. Casualties were even higher at Gettysburg, the three-day conflict that holds the tragic record for the most Americans killed and wounded in a single battle. It can also be pointed out that some Confederate generals, especially Lee and Johnston, often continued fighting long after their cause was hopeless, no matter how heavy the losses were. Lee, in particular, must share with Grant great responsibility for the tragic toll of the Civil War.

There is evidence to suggest that Grant was not uncaring about the men killed or wounded by his orders. But he would not allow compassion to cloud his strategy. He displayed a remarkable ability to focus on the task at hand, shoving everything else out of his mind. One incident especially dramatizes this single-mindedness of purpose: In May 1864, a Union officer recalled watching Grant write a battle report. He was sitting on a fallen tree when a Rebel artillery shell exploded a few feet in front of him, spraying mud and shell fragments in all directions. Grant looked up for a moment, then returned to writing his dispatch.

Similarly, in a famous description of him, Union Colonel Theodore Lyman wrote: "He has three expressions: deep thought; extreme determination; and a great simplicity and calmness. . . He habitually wears an expression as if he had determined to drive his head through a brick wall and was about to do it." Mary Chestnut observed the same characteristic from her Confederate perspective: "He fights to win, that chap does. He is not distracted by a thousand side issues; he does not see them. He is narrow and sure—sees only in a straight line. . . ."

87

# When Did the Civil War End?

Many Americans consider the date of Lee's surrender to Grant at Appomattox Court House—April 9, 1865—the official date that the Civil War came to an end. Technically, however, that date marks only the date when Lee surrendered his Army of Northern Virginia to Grant.

At the time there were several large Confederate armies still in the field, as well as thousands of guerillas who supported the Confederate cause operating across the South. To make matters more complicated, when Lee surrendered, Confederate President Jefferson Davis and some of his cabinet were on a train heading toward Mississippi. Davis and many of the Rebels in the field were far from giving up. It would take another month for all fighting to cease. In fact, the war came very close to turning into a guerilla conflict that could have lasted a generation or more.

Of the Confederate armies in the field after April 9, General Joseph Johnston's force in North Carolina was the most formidable. These Rebels had halted the northward march of Union General William Sherman, whose men had laid waste to much of Georgia and South Carolina. Lee was attempting to join Johnston when he was trapped by Grant. After Lee's surrender, Johnston held out for two weeks before lack of supplies and constant Union pressure forced him to ask Sherman for terms of surrender. Like his good friend Grant, Sherman was a brutal warrior but a kind victor. He offered terms to Johnston similar to those Grant offered Lee.

Meanwhile, Confederate President Davis was ordering all remaining Rebel units to disperse into the dense backwoods of the South and continue the war as hit-and-run guerrillas. A number of well-known Southern commanders had already demonstrated great skill in this type of fighting. In the Deep South, General Nathan Bedford Forrest had so tormented Sherman's troops that Sherman called him "the devil." In the Shenandoah Valley, Colonel John Mosby led so many successful raids that he became known as "The Gray Ghost."

Forrest and Mosby, as well as many other Rebels, could have prolonged the war for months or years had they followed Davis' orders. In the end, however, they, like Lee and Johnston, felt the South has already suffered too much. In early May, shortly before Davis was captured by Union cavalry, Forrest, Mosby, and the majority of the Rebels in the field surrendered. The last Confederate force to surrender did so in late June, 1865. These Confederates were led by General Stand Watie, a Cherokee chief, who had led a Native American force of Rebels into more than a dozen battles in the West.

# Chapter 4

## POSTSCRIPT: THE GENERAL IN POLITICS

The assassination of Abraham Lincoln threw the nation into turmoil. Even as his funeral train wound its way through the countryside to his home state of Illinois, the "Radical" Republicans were calling for revenge and punishment of the South. In the weeks before his death, Lincoln had urged a policy of reconciliation. His advice to Grant and Sherman in accepting Rebel surrenders was simple: "Let 'em down easy." The Radical Republicans in Congress ignored their fallen leader and went ahead with a harsh program of "Radical Reconstruction." They divided the defeated South into five military districts, for example, and the last troops were not withdrawn for ten years. When President Johnson, a Democrat, defied the Radicals, he was impeached, and spared removal from office by a single vote.

OPPOSITE: Grant takes the oath of office in 1869.

To the Republicans, General Grant was a great hero, and a man who fit their agenda. In 1866, they rewarded him by naming him a full general, a position that had previously been held only by George Washington. In 1868, the Republicans rewarded him again with their nomination for the presidency.

Grant served two terms as president, accepting the office as the thanks of a grateful nation. He knew, however, that he brought few political skills to the highest office in the land. In fact, he brought two serious liabilities. First, he did not believe that the function of the president was to lead, but rather simply to carry out the laws passed by Congress. In accepting the nomination in 1868, he said, "I shall have no policy of my own to enforce against the will of the people." And he meant "will of the people" as expressed by their representatives in Congress. This philosophy was unfortunate at a time when strong leadership might have united a country still fiercely divided by the war.

Grant's second liability stemmed from his personality—he simply trusted people too much. And he continued to trust them long after they had betrayed him. The result was that the two Grant administrations, from 1869 to 1877, were riddled with scandals. None of the scandals touched President Grant personally, but he remained blind to the criminal actions of those closest to him.

The decade following the Civil War was a time of rapid change. Americans were pushing into the Western frontier. The economy, swept along by the innovations of the Industrial Revolution, seemed to offer endless opportunities for new wealth. A good deal of that wealth was finding its way into the pockets of men in government—state, local, and federal officials. In this wide open, anything-goes atmosphere, a number of men close to Grant were eager to claim their fair share of the wealth to be had.

For example, Grant's first vice-president, Schuyler Colfax, was mixed up in a scheme that involved a company called Creit Mobiliér—a firm that was contracted to do the construction work on the transcontinental railroad. The officers of the company, however, were charging their stockholders millions of dollars more than the work cost. The scandal got even uglier when the officials tried to sell stock to members of Congress at ridiculously low prices in the hopes of avoiding an investigation. A congressional committee eventually did investigate and exposed the fraud. It was Grant's poor luck that the scandal, which had its origins before he was elected, was exposed while he was in office.

In another scheme, two of America's most notorious crooks—Jay Gould and "Jubilee Jim" Fisk—decided they would corner the market in

★
The transcontinental railroad was completed when tracks from East and West were joined in Utah in 1869.
★

93

gold. When scarcity made the price of gold go high enough, they would sell and reap huge profits. Their scheme, however, would only work if the Treasury Department did not put the government's gold certificates on the market to hold the price down. To keep the Treasury out of it, Gould and Fisk hired the president's brother-in-law A.R. Corbin. Through Corbin, Gould and Fisk met the president. They wined and dined Grant royally and the president was both flattered and impressed with their successful business air. They convinced him that, if the Treasury released gold, the depressed prices would be ruinous to farm families. The scheme proceeded far enough by September 1869, that it touched off a stock market panic. Grant finally saw what was happening and ordered the Treasury to release gold. The scheme collapsed but not before hundreds of investors had been hurt. This was yet another affair that made President Grant look incompetent.

Vice-President Henry Wilson

By 1872, many voters were fed up, but Grant was easily swept into office for a second term. The scandals continued. His secretary of the treasury was involved in a scheme for the collection of delinquent taxes, keeping most of the money that was collected. Secretary of War William Belknap sold Indian trading posts on government reservations to the highest bidder. His private secretary Orville Babcock was part of a "Whiskey Ring" that cheated the government out of millions of tax dollars. Grant repeatedly made things worse by standing up for the men involved in each scheme. He testified on Babcock's behalf, for example, and then, after the dust cleared, brought him back to the White House as "inspector of lighthouses."

In his last annual message in December, 1876, Grant spoke with his usual humility: "It was my fortune, or misfortune, to be called to the office of Chief Executive, without any previous political training. . . . Under such circumstances it is but reasonable to suppose that errors of judgment must have occurred. . . Failures have been errors of judgment, not of intent." One of his biographers, F. Norton Boothe, was not as charitable: "It was, in fact, a national disgrace. Historian Bruce Catton echoes that his eight years were "a pretty sorry time."

Although Grant's presidency is considered largely a series of embarrassing failures, there were some positive achievements to be noted.

Schuyler Colfax

95

The Grant administration established a basis for settling disputes with England, established a more humane Indian policy, reformed the civil service bureaucracy, and helped the nation weather the stormy post-Civil War years of rebuilding known as Reconstruction.

Perhaps the most surprising thing about Grant's presidency was that he actually enjoyed it; so did Julia and the children. Their eight years in the White House represented the longest time they had ever spent in one place. The saddest part of their stay in the White House, they said, was when they had to leave.

## The Final Challenge

Soon after Grant left office, he, Julia, and their youngest son, Jesse, set sail for Europe. Grant had little money. Presidents did not receive pensions in those days, and he had been forced to resign from the army to run for office. With the help of some friends, the Grants could indulge their love of travel. In England, the former president was hailed as a hero of war and peace and was invited to dine with Queen Victoria. Next, they toured Europe at a leisurely pace, then headed for the Middle East and Asia. They received the same hero's welcome everywhere. Not surprisingly, the Grants stretched out their world tour for two years.

Back in the United States, leading Republicans failed in their attempts to push Grant for a third presidential term in 1880. In 1881, the Grants moved from Galena, Illinois, to New York City, where he once again experienced business difficulties. There, Grant lent his name to a Wall Street investment firm, and persuaded some family members to join. Within three years, Grant was flat broke, having been defrauded by his business partners. New York millionaire William Vanderbilt had to provide the money for Grant to pay his household expenses.

In order to pay some of his debts, Grant wrote an article for *Century* Magazine on the Battle of Shiloh. It was a great success. Readers were impressed by his clear, vivid writing style, and publishers were eager to publish his memoirs. Grant's friend, author and humorist Mark Twain, insisted that he himself would be the publisher.

Twain's support gave Grant confidence, and he set to work. The prospect of putting his life experiences down on paper was exciting to him, and he was determined to make enough money to settle his debts and provide for comfortable years of retirement. The literary project, however, quickly became a race against time. Grant learned that he was dying of throat cancer, undoubtedly caused by his years of cigar smoking. Throughout the war, he had watched countless men die with courage and dignity. His friends and family knew

97

he would face his own death with the same dignity.

As the pages of his manuscript piled up, his health deteriorated. Doctors first said he had months to live, then weeks, finally days. His penmanship became harder and harder to read; his body was regularly wracked with pain. But he would not stop or give up hope. Julia, always with him, took him to a cabin in the Adirondacks for the fresh air and comfort. Grant rallied long enough to scrawl several versions of the final pages that would be *The Personal Memoir of Ulysses S. Grant* in two volumes. He died quietly 48 hours later, on July 23, 1885, knowing he had finished his final campaign.

Twain began publication of the two volumes right away, completing the task in 1886. It is still regarded today as one of the best autobiographies in American literature. Sales of the memoir provided Julia and the family with a comfortable fortune. That final triumph typified Grant's life, and especially his military career. With that great determination and the single-minded ability to block out every distraction, he had achieved what he set out to do, knowing from the start that he would accept nothing short of victory.

In many ways, it is difficult to evaluate a person as famous and controversial as Ulysses Grant over the course of his entire life. Like most people, he

> ★
>
> Mark Twain, author of *Tom Sawyer* and *Huckleberry Finn*, supported the Confederacy during the Civil War.
>
> ★

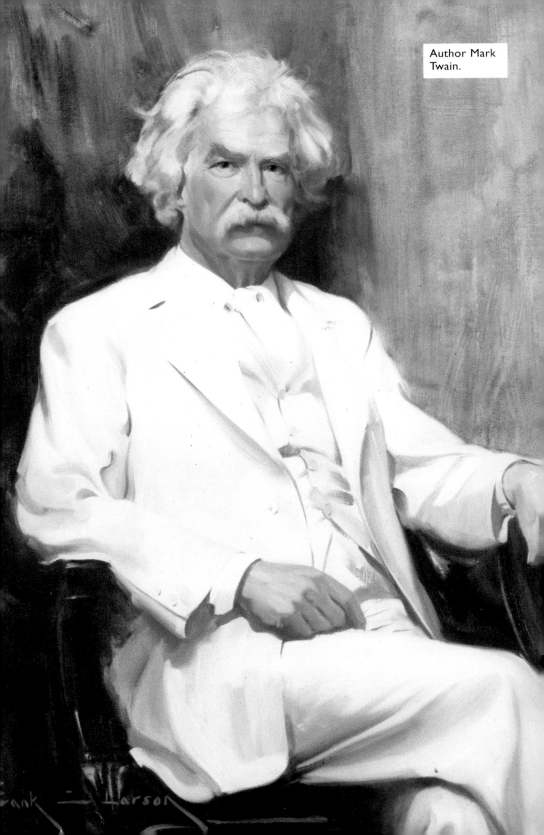

Author Mark Twain.

had strong and weak points. He was a store clerk who gave the Union its first victories in the Civil War. He was the general who won that war—at an almost unimaginable cost. He was also a disastrous president—who was re-elected to a second term and almost ran for a third.

Perhaps it would be most useful to evaluate Grant based on one single moment in time: April 9, 1865. In that moment, an unkempt, cigar-smoking, forty-three-year-old man sat down with a man nearing sixty, the perfect image of a military commander. Both men have given orders resulting in the deaths of hundreds of thousands of young men. Now the younger man had won.

It all could have ended very differently. Had Grant been bitter and bent on revenge, many would have understood his harsh treatment of the beaten Confederates. He had lost again and again to Lee, and because of those losses had been called a "butcher" and worse. Now, he had a chance to bring the elegant Southerner to his knees. Instead, Ulysses Grant chose to be generous and respectful. He offered surrender terms that Lee gratefully accepted. He would not allow celebration by his men, choosing to honor his worthy opponent instead. With these gestures, Ulysses Grant did all that was in his power to make our nation whole once again—and, in so doing, achieved greatness.

# Glossary

**armistice**  an agreement to stop fighting between opponents in order to discuss peace terms.

**artillery**  large weapons used by fighting forces that fall into three categories—guns or cannons, howitzers, and mortars.

**brigade**  a military unit smaller that a division, usually consisting of three to five regiments of 500 to 1,000 soldiers.

**bunkers**  small sand holes or pits.

**casualties**  the total number of soldiers dead, wounded, and missing after a battle.

**commander**  a military leader, usually holding the rank of general.

**corps**  a military grouping of between 10,000 and 20,000 soldiers.

**division**  a military grouping of between 6,000 and 8,000 soldiers or two to three brigades.

**emancipation**  freedom.

**flotilla**  a small fleet of ships.

**ford**  a crossing on a stream or river.

**plantation**  a large farm in the South worked by slaves in the years before the parapets.

**regiment**  a military unit smaller than a brigade or a division. In the Civil War soldiers fought in the same regiment throughout the war, with fellow soldiers who usually from the same state, city, or town.

**reinforce** in military terms, to strengthen a military unit by sending in fresh troops.

**secede** to break away.

**siege** the surrounding and blockading of a city, town, or fortress by an army attempting to capture it.

**skirmishes** minor or preliminary conflicts or disputes.

**typhoid** an often-fatal disease caused by contaminated drinking water.

## For More Information

### Web Sites

*Ulysses Grant: A Guide for Students*
**http://saints.css.edu/mkelsey/student.html**
An excellent starting point for links to photos, a biography, and other web sites about Grant

*Ulysses Grant Home Page*
**http://www.mscomm.com/~ulysses/**
An excellent source for virtually every aspect of Grant's life: Interviews with those who knew him at various times, Grant's own writing, a collection of his paintings, and much more

*Ulysses Grant Photo Gallery*
**http://www.mscomm.com/~ulysses/page150.html**
A fine collection of both well-known and unpublished photos of Grant from the Civil War through his presidency

102

## Books

Archer, Jules. *A House Divided: Ulysses Grant and Robert E Lee*. New York, Scholastic 1994. A book that examines the path each man took leading to Appomattox.

Boothe, Norton. *Ulysses S. Grant. Great American Generals Series*. London, 1990. Brief, illustrated overview focuses mainly on his role in the Civil War.

Catton, Bruce. *U.S. Grant and the American Military Tradition*. New York, 1954. For slightly older students who would like a more detailed reading of Grant's life and military career.

Frost, Lawrence A. *U.S. Grant Album: a Pictorial Biography of Ulysses S. Grant*. Seattle, 1966. A biography with a large collection of photographs.

Kent, Zachary. *Ulysses S. Grant. Encyclopedia of Presidents Series*. Chicago, 1989. An indexed overview of Grant's life.

## Index